For the Teacher

This reproducible study guide consists of lessons to use in conjunction with a specific novel. Used together, the books and the guide provide an exciting supplement to the basal reader in your classroom. Written in chapter-by-chapter format, the guide contains a synopsis, pre-reading activities, vocabulary and comprehension exercises, as well as extension activities to be used as follow-up to the novel.

In a homogeneous classroom, whole class instruction with one title is appropriate. In a heterogeneous classroom, reading groups should be formed: each group works on a different novel on its reading level. Depending upon the length of time devoted to reading in the classroom, each novel, with its guide and accompanying lessons, may be completed in three to six weeks.

Begin using NOVEL-TIES for reading development by distributing the novel and a folder to each child. Distribute duplicated pages of the study guide for students to place in their folders. After examining the cover and glancing through the book, students can participate in several pre-reading activities. Vocabulary questions should be considered prior to reading a chapter; all other work should be done after the chapter has been read. Comprehension questions can be answered orally or in writing. The classroom teacher should determine the amount of work to be assigned, always keeping in mind that readers must be nurtured and that the ultimate goal is encouraging students' love of reading.

The benefits of using NOVEL-TIES are numerous. Students read good literature in the original, rather than in abridged or edited form. The good reading habits, formed by practice in focusing on interpretive comprehension and literary techniques, will be transferred to the books students read independently. Passive readers become active, avid readers.

Novel-Ties® are printed on recycled paper.

SYNOPSIS

This novel begins in June 1941 in Vilna, Poland. Ten-year-old Esther Rudomin happily lives with her parents in the home of her paternal grandparents. Once an affluent Jewish family, the Rudomins have seen many ominous changes in the years since Hitler invaded Poland in 1939. The town is under the occupation of the Russians, who have confiscated the family business and property.

On a day that is to change Esther's life, Russian soldiers come to the house and arrest the family for being "capitalists." They are taken from their home and herded into cramped cattle cars. Even worse, Esther's grandfather is torn from his family and forced to board another train.

After a long and arduous journey, the Rudomins find themselves in Siberia, where the adults are forced to work in a gypsum mine while Esther and the other children weed potato fields. When amnesty is granted to the Polish prisoners, the family moves to barracks near the village of Rubtsovsk, where they meet old friends from Vilna, the Kaftals. Esther's mother is assigned to work in a bakery, while her father serves as bookkeeper at a construction job. Food is scarce and the life is hard. Soon the Rudomins and Kaftals find shelter in town in the crowded hut of a Russian peasant couple.

Esther's joy at being able to attend school is dampened by a strict teacher named Raisa Nikitovna and the unfriendly girl, Svetlana, with whom she must share books. Having little food and few clothes, the family finds themselves ill-prepared for the harsh Siberian winter. To add to their suffering, news reaches them of the death of Esther's grandfather.

When the seven deportees are forced to leave the hut, they find shelter in a miserable hut occupied by two dour sisters and a child. One day Esther's father is detained and interrogated by the dreaded secret police, a warning that the family is living under very precarious circumstances.

When spring comes, life improves somewhat for Esther, who gets an invitation to go to the movies and finally makes friends with Svetlana after cutting off the braids that the Russian girl had envied. When the family gets permission to move into a dilapidated and unoccupied hut, they fix it up and leave the Kaftals, who elect to stay with the dour sisters.

The family is devastated when Esther's father is ordered to work in a labor brigade near the front lines. With food and fuel in short supply, Esther first steals coal and wood shavings and then does knitting in exchange for food and supplies. Two new friends, Uncle Yozia and Aunt Zaya, help the family by getting Esther and her mother a temporary position caring for a tractor factory director at his home while his wife is away. When this position ends, Esther and her mother move to another hut, this time occupied by a young couple and their baby.

Esther becomes preoccupied preparing for a declamation contest. When Raisa Nikitovna turns Esther away from the contest because she has no shoes, Esther races home to put on a pair of her mother's ill-fitting slippers. Returning to the contest weary and dispirited, she gives a disappointing performance. Things improve, however, for Esther when Uncle Yozia registers her in a new school, where she excels under the tutelage of exceptional teachers.

News of German atrocities brings fear for the family the Rudomins left behind in Poland. When the war finally ends, the Rudomins find out that almost all of their family have been killed in concentration camps. Ironically, exile to Siberia saved the deportees from the same fate.

Esther's father, released from the labor brigade, writes to the family from Poland. Esther's mother looks forward to the day when she can join him there, but Esther, now fifteen, fears leaving the place she now considers home. Esther enters another declamation contest, hoping to redeem herself, but the family leaves for Poland days before the contest is to take place.

Taking the same cattle cars back to their homeland, the deportees leave Siberia. When they arrive in Lodz, they are shocked by the devastation all around them. Esther, however, is thrilled when she catches the first glimpse of her father from the train. The family is reunited, and their exile is over.

BACKGROUND INFORMATION

On August 23, 1939, the Nazis and Soviets signed a pact of nonaggression which provided for the division of Poland between Germany and Russia. Having assured Soviet neutrality, Adolph Hitler, the German dictator, felt free to attack Poland on September 1, 1939, thus starting World War II. The Poles were unable to withstand the surprise attack of Germany's motorized armies and powerful air force. On September 17, the situation worsened when Soviet troops attacked Poland from the east.

Within Poland the people suffered cruel persecution by the Soviets and the Nazis. In alarming numbers Poland's Jewish population and intellectual elite were stripped of their land and possessions, deported, detained in forced labor and concentration camps, and even exterminated. In fact, Hitler's goal for the entire European Jewish population was nothing short of genocide, extermination of the entire people.

The Soviets exiled many of their political prisoners, like the Rudomin family in this book, to Siberia, the part of the Soviet Union lying east of the Ural Mountains. Although Siberian winters are brutal, with some of the lowest temperatures in the world, temperatures of 90° F. – 100° F. are common on midsummer days in central Siberia. The area portrayed in the novel is the great West Siberian Lowland, the western third of Siberia lying between the Urals and the Yenisey River. Much of this area consists of steppes—vast, treeless plains.

The 1930s witnessed the spread of concentration and forced labor camps in Siberia. When the Germans invaded the Soviet Union during World War II, much Soviet industry was transferred to the Urals and Siberia, which together became the industrial backbone of the Soviet war effort.

After Germany attacked Russia in June 1941, the Polish government in exile concluded a pact with the Soviet Union on July 30, 1941. One of the provisions of this pact was that all Polish war prisoners and deportees were to be released. The Soviet government, however, did not live up to this agreement and released only a fraction of the Poles being held in the Soviet Union. Those who were released from forced labor camps were compelled to remain in Siberia until the end of the war, when repatriation—the process of sending refugees back to their own country—could begin.

GLOSSARY

anti-Semite	person who shows dislike or hatred of Jews
bania	public bath (Russian)
baracholka	marketplace (Russian)
challah	ritual bread
fufaika	quilted jacket worn in Siberia
Kaddish	prayer for the dead
rabbi	ordained preacher and teacher of Jewish law and religion, usually serving as the spiritual leader of a Jewish congregation
Sabbath	seventh day of the Jewish week (Saturday) set aside for rest and worship
sapogy	knee-high leather boots worn by the well-to-do in Siberia
sit *shivah*	sit in mourning for a period, usually seven days, during which Jewish mourners receive condolence visits from family and friends
Sh'mah Israel	beginning of a prayer (Hear, O Israel . . .)
synagogue	Jewish house of worship
Talmudic scholar	one who studies the Talmud, a collection of sixty-three volumes containing the Jewish civil and canonical law in the form of interpretation and expansion of the teachings of the Old Testament
yahrzeit	candle
	memorial candle for the dead
yarmulka	skullcap worn by Jewish men and boys, especially for prayer and ceremonial occasions
Yiddish	language which originally developed from a dialect of Middle High German, containing many Hebrew and Slavic words, and written in Hebrew characters; spoken mainly by Jews of eastern and central Europe and their descendants

PRE-READING ACTIVITIES

1. In *The Endless Steppe* the Rudomin family is exiled to Siberia in 1941. Brainstorm with your classmates to fill in a K-W-L chart on Siberia, such as the one below. Jot down what you already know in the first column. List your questions in the second column. After you read each chapter, record what you have learned in the third column.

Siberia		
What We Know K	What We Want To Know W	What We Learned L

2. **Social Studies Connection:** Read the Background Information on page two of this study guide and do some additional research to learn more about Polish Jews who were exiled to Siberia during World War II. Find out what happened to the Jews who remained in Poland during the war. As you read the book, consider in what ways the Rudomins might be considered "lucky" to have been in Siberia during the war years.

3. **Social Studies Connection:** Do some research to learn about the Russian Revolution. Find out why the Tsarist regime was overthrown and what were the original ideals of the Communist revolutionaries. As you read this book, notice how life in Soviet Russia differed from these ideals.

4. **Cooperative Learning Activity:** Work with a small cooperative learning group to discuss the meaning of the word "home." What does the word mean to you? To what extent is it people who make a home? To what extent is home a place? What would you miss most about your home if you were suddenly forced to leave?

5. In this novel, a young girl must adjust to many changes in her life. What was the most important change you ever had to adjust to in your life? What do you think was most important in helping you with your adjustment? What did you learn from the experience?

6. Have you read any other books of fiction set in Europe during World War II? If so, when and where were these stories set? What did you learn about life at that time?

7. This book is autobiographical, based on the author's own life. What advantages are there in writing a book about your own life? What are the drawbacks? If you had to choose a period of your life to write about, what would it be?

8. **Social Studies Connection:** As you read, create a time line from 1935 through 1945, filling in important historical events relating to the war in Europe. Use events mentioned in the novel as well as significant events you find in an encyclopedia or history book.

9. **Social Studies Connection:** Look at a map or globe to find the location and action of the novel. As you read the book, trace the route the family takes from Vilna to Siberia.

CHAPTERS 1, 2

Vocabulary: Draw a line from each word on the left to its definition on the right. Then use the numbered words to fill in the blanks in the sentences below.

1. opulent	a. warning
2. aberration	b. smelling very bad
3. explicit	c. temporary mental disorder
4. admonishing	d. in an exacting manner
5. fastidiously	e. showing wealth
6. immaculate	f. secretly
7. surreptitiously	g. continuously
8. fetid	h. clearly expressed
9. sardonic	i. flawless
10. incessantly	j. bitterly mocking

· ·

1. The _____ air in the small cabin forced us outside.

2. My room, which is usually in _____ order, was in total disarray after the party.

3. When you go for a job interview, it is best to be _____ groomed from head to toe.

4. To impress their neighbors, the family built the most _____ house on the block.

5. The prisoners were _____ hungry because they were fed only thin soup and bread.

6. The child _____ reached for a cookie when his parents weren't looking.

7. After walking in the desert for two days without water, we worried that the lake we saw in the distance was a(n) _____.

8. If you give me _____ directions, I will have no trouble finding your house.

9. After the teacher made a(n) _____ comment about my expressed opinion, I no longer spoke up in class.

10. I cast a(n) _____ glance at my friend so she would not reveal our hiding places, but I was too late.

Chapters 1, 2 (cont.)

Questions:

1. Why did Esther enjoy living in Vilna before the day the Russian soldiers arrived?

2. How had life changed for Esther's family once Hitler's armies invaded Poland?

3. Why did Russian soldiers come to Esther's house on a morning in June 1941?

4. Why did Esther's mother forbid her to take the photo albums?

5. What event caused Esther's grandmother to let out a "dreadful scream" at the railroad station? What uncharacteristic behavior did Grandmother exhibit after this event?

6. What were Esther's first impressions of the cattle cars?

7. How did the different members of the Rudomin family deal with the ordeal of the first night in the cattle car?

8. What character trait did Esther's mother reveal when she refused to let Esther accept food from the peasants on the train?

9. How did the conditions in the cattle cars worsen?

10. How long did the journey in the cattle car last? How did the people react when they finally reached their destination?

Questions for Discussion:

1. Why did the photo album become Esther's "most important possession"? Do you have any photographs that are particularly important to you?

2. "Tears were against the rules" in Esther's house. Do you think that a family should hide their sorrows from one another? In what way, if any, might tears help Esther's family cope with their situation?

3. Why do you think the passengers on board the cattle car accepted the authority of Esther's father?

4. Do you think Esther's mother was right to refuse food for her daughter?

5. Do you think Esther's memories of Vilna were realistic or became enhanced over time?

Literary Element: Setting

Setting refers to the place and time in which the events in a work of fiction occur. What is the setting of the novel?

_____

How important do you think the setting will be to this story?

_____

_____

Chapters 1, 2 (cont.)

Literary Devices:

I.   *Point of View* — In literature, the point of view refers to the voice telling the story. It could be the author narrating the story or one of the characters. From whose point of view is this story told?

_____

II. *Hook* — A hook in literature refers to material at the beginning of a book whose purpose it is to capture the reader's attention. What is the hook at the beginning of this book?

_____

_____

Writing Activity:

Imagine that you are Esther's mother. Write a journal entry describing your thoughts and feelings about the events that have taken place in your life since being arrested by the Russians. Be sure to explain why you think it is important not to cry.

CHAPTERS 3 - 5

Vocabulary: Synonyms are words with similar meanings. Draw a line from each word in column A to its synonym in column B. Then use the words in column A to fill in the blanks in the sentences below.

A	B
1. cataclysm	a. respect
2. bucolic	b. accidentally
3. austere	c. hinted
4. deference	d. rural
5. demeaning	e. restricted
6. circumscribed	f. conspicuously
7. inadvertently	g. disaster
8. malevolent	h. stern
9. insinuated	i. humiliating
10. ostentatiously	j. spiteful

· ·

1. Against the _____ background of our family home, no one played or laughed aloud.

2. Hoping to win the event at any cost, the athlete _____ that his rival was competing unfairly.

3. People should show _____ to those who are older and wiser.

4. Atomic war between nations would be a(n) _____.

5. The girl led such a(n) _____ life that she knew little about what was going on in the world around her.

6. If you consider the tasks involved in running a household to be _____, you must be able to afford to hire someone else to do them for you.

7. Wishing to be closer to nature, I left the city for the _____ life.

8. The accident occurred when the driver _____ stepped on the accelerator instead of the brake.

9. The child _____ held her nose to show that she didn't like the food put in front of her.

10. The _____ glare from his rival made the athlete very uneasy.

Chapters 3 - 5 (cont.)

Questions:

1. Describe the village of Rubtsovsk and the surrounding land.

2. How did Esther react when she learned that she was in Siberia? Why did she react this way?

3. Contrast Popravka and Makrinin in their treatment of the prisoners.

4. Why did Esther conclude that her family was luckier than many others who had come to Rubtsovsk?

5. What kindness was shown to the prisoners first by the water boy and then by two young village girls? How did this affect the prisoners?

6. What kind of work did each member of the family do? Why couldn't Makrinin offer them more appropriate work?

7. Why did Esther enjoy the *baracholka* so much?

8. In what ways were Esther and her grandmother alike?

Questions for Discussion;

1. Why do you think that Popravka treated the prisoners with such scorn?

2. Why do you think that laughter was especially important to the prisoners? How important is laughter in your life?

Social Studies Connection:

1. The Rudomins were arrested by a communist government for being capitalists. Do some research to find out the difference between capitalism and communism. Why do you think that the communists felt it important to arrest people they considered capitalists?

2. Esther sees portraits of Lenin, Stalin, Marx, and Engels in the converted school building. Do some research to learn about these men and the role they played in the history of Russia.

Chapters 3 - 5 (cont.)

Literary Devices:

I. *Simile* — A simile is a figure of speech in which a comparison between two unlike objects is stated directly using the words "like" or "as." For example:

> The lightning would fork out like a malevolent claw in a frenzy to ground itself on the treeless steppe.

What is being compared?

_____

In what way does this comparison help the reader visualize the scene?

_____

II. *Metaphor* — A metaphor is a figure of speech in which a comparison between two unlike objects is suggested or implied. For example:

> . . . our life was so circumscribed that most of the people around us were only figures on a lantern slide seen without narration.

What is being compared?

_____

Why is this an apt comparison?

_____

_____

Writing Activity:

Sensory images are vivid descriptions that appeal to the senses. The scene describing the *baracholka* includes many sensory images. Try to find a phrase that describes each sense, and list it along with the page number on the chart below.

Senses	Phrase	Page
Sound		
Smell		
Sight		
Taste		
Touch		

Now use phrases that appeal to the senses to describe an event in your life. You could describe a vacation, a sporting event, a picnic, or any event that involves different senses.

CHAPTERS 6, 7

Vocabulary: Use the context to determine the meaning of the underlined word in each sentence. Then find the exact meaning in a dictionary.

1. The United States government granted <u>amnesty</u> to those who left the country rather than serve in the Vietnam War.

   Your definition _____

   Dictionary definition _____

2. I supplemented the small <u>stipend</u> I received for teaching night school with tutoring jobs.

   Your definition _____

   Dictionary definition _____

3. Although she dislikes me, my opponent <u>hypocritically</u> congratulated me on my win.

   Your definition _____

   Dictionary definition _____

4. Wanting to make a good impression, I gave my new boss my most <u>ingratiating</u> smile.

   Your definition _____

   Dictionary definition _____

5. Our <u>indulgent</u> teacher praised every poem we wrote.

   Your definition _____

   Dictionary definition _____

6. The poisonous cleaning fluids and other household solutions had been <u>inaccessibly</u> stored away so that the young children could not reach them.

   Your definition _____

   Dictionary definition _____

7. The private detective kept a detailed <u>dossier</u> on the man she was investigating.

   Your definition _____

   Dictionary definition _____

8. At the press conference, the President was hit with a <u>barrage</u> of questions.

   Your definition _____

   Dictionary definition _____

Chapters 6, 7 (cont.)

Questions:

1. How did the Rudomins' life change after amnesty was granted? In what way did their life remain the same?

2. What did Esther mean when she said that Anya Kaftal "had transformed vanity into an act of courage"?

3. What "luxuries" did the family find in their new home in the barracks that they did not have at the mine?

4. Why did Esther want her family to move to the village?

5. Why did Nina refuse to believe that the Rudomins were Jews? What did this suggest about her?

6. How did Esther feel about the first snowfall? Why didn't her parents feel the same way?

7. In what ways did school turn out to be a disappointment for Esther?

8. How was the curriculum at the school Esther attended in Siberia a product of the Russian Revolution?

Questions for Discussion:

1. Who do you think stole the bread?

2. Compare and contrast the Siberian school with your own.

3. What personal characteristics do you think were required to survive life as a deportee in Siberia?

Science Connection:

Esther's mother was worried because Nikita had trachoma. Do some research to find out more about this disease.

Literary Device: Foreshadowing

Foreshadowing refers to the clues an author provides to suggest what may happen later in the novel. What do you think the author might be foreshadowing in the last paragraph of Chapter Seven?

Writing Activity:

Imagine you are Esther and write a journal entry describing your thoughts and feelings after your first day at school in Siberia.

CHAPTERS 8 - 11

Vocabulary: Use the words in the Word Box and the clues below to complete the crossword puzzle.

WORD BOX				
amenities	cajole	dexterously	dour	egregious
incongruously	infirmary	largesse	obliterating	pariah
paroxysms	pilfering	reminiscent	superfluous	taciturn

Across

1. sudden, severe attacks of the symptoms of a disease
4. skillfully
10. generous gift
11. place for the care of the sick or injured
12. stealing
13. inappropriately
14. remarkably or extraordinarily bad

Down

2. polite acts
3. unnecessary
4. gloomy or stern
5. speaking very little
6. blotting out
7. coax
8. awakening memories of something similar
9. outcast

Chapters 8 - 11 (cont.)

Questions:

1. How did Esther and Grandmother discover who took the missing food? Why did Grandmother cover up the crime?

2. What prevented Esther from going to school? How would you describe the doctor who cared for Esther?

3. What was Esther's "first personal confrontation with tragedy"? How was this sad time made even more difficult for the family?

4. Why did the Rudomins have to move from Nina and Nikita's hut? Why was it even more difficult now to find housing?

5. Why was the Rudomin's new home with the "dour sisters" worse than the one before?

6. What happened to make Esther very proud of her father and very frightened for him?

7. What two occurrences helped make Esther feel less like an outsider?

8. Why did the Rudomins leave the hut of the dour sisters? Why did Esther describe their new hut as "heaven"?

9. What transformation took place in Vanya the bum? What accounted for this transformation?

Questions for Discussion:

1. Why do you think that Mrs. Kaftal stole food instead of asking for it? What would you have done in her situation?

2. Do you think that Esther should have cut her hair?

3. Why do you think it was so important to Grandmother that Esther become an archive of her past?

4. Why do you think that Ivan Petrovich left so suddenly without even saying goodbye?

Social Studies Connection:

What did you learn in this book about religious observance under the Soviet regime? Do some research to learn about the major religion in Russia prior to the Revolution and the way Jews were treated historically.

Chapters 8 - 11 (cont.)

Math Connection:

Esther needs four rubles to go to the movies. The ruble is the monetary unit of Russia. Find out what a ruble is equivalent to in United States money. What would four rubles be worth in the United States today?

Literary Device: Personification

Personification is a literary device in which an author grants human qualities to nonhuman objects, animals, and ideas. For example:

> Trouble was our constant dark companion.

What is being personified?

_____

How is this more effective than if the author had said, "We had many troubles"?

_____

_____

Writing Activity:

Imagine you are Ivan Petrovich and write a letter of explanation telling the Rudomins why it was necessary to leave.

CHAPTERS 12 - 15

Vocabulary: Use a word from the Word Box to replace each underlined word or phrase in the following sentences. Write the word on the line below the sentence.

WORD BOX			
atrocities	degradation	infraction	magnitude
nondescript	opaque	revulsion	woebegone

1. We could not find the courthouse because it stood in a group of <u>not easily classified</u> buildings.

   _____

2. You will suffer <u>disgrace</u> if you are caught cheating.

   _____

3. Rescue operations were slow to arrive because the state had never before seen a hurricane of this <u>degree</u>.

   _____

4. The <u>sorrowful</u> child could not get over the loss of her pet.

   _____

5. The Germans committed <u>very cruel and brutal acts</u> during World War II.

   _____

6. Robbery is an <u>offense</u> punishable by law.

   _____

7. I was disappointed when my mother's <u>hard to understand</u> expression didn't offer me the praise I desired.

   _____

8. I felt <u>disgust</u> when I saw the man beating his dog.

   _____

Chapters 12 - 15 (cont.)

Questions:

1. What duties did the Siberian children perform other than going to school?

2. What "tragic" news did a letter for Esther's father bring? How did each member of the family react to this news?

3. What was the family's greatest concern when Father left?

4. How did Esther supplement the family's fuel supply? Why didn't her mother and grandmother stop her from doing this?

5. Why did Esther's mother make her a birthday party? Why was it a bittersweet occasion for the family?

6. Why did Mother and Grandmother begin to have "deep concern" about the family back in Poland? What specific regret did Esther's mother have?

7. Why did Esther think the loss of thirty rubles was a tragedy for the family?

8. When Esther took up knitting, who was her first customer? How did Esther feel after completing the job?

9. How did Marya Nikolayevna take advantage of Esther? What did this suggest about Marya's character?

Questions for Discussion:

1. When news came that Father had to leave, the family was "exhausted by emotion both expressed and unexpressed." How do you think unexpressed emotions could be exhausting?

2. Esther's mother made a birthday party for her daughter even though it meant using up precious food. Do you think that the birthday party was a good idea?

3. Do you think Esther's mother should have asked Yozia and Zaya for help? Do you think her pride was justified?

Music Connection:

Svetlana played the balalaika. Learn about this instrument and locate pictures of it. Then try to obtain some recordings of the balalaika to play for the class.

Chapters 12 - 15 (cont.)

Literary Element: Characterization

The reader learns about characters by what they say, do, and think and by what others say about them. Working with a partner, use the Venn diagram below to compare the characters of Esther's mother and father. List the ways they are alike in the overlapping part of the circles. When you have completed the diagram, discuss the traits you believe Esther inherited from each of her parents.

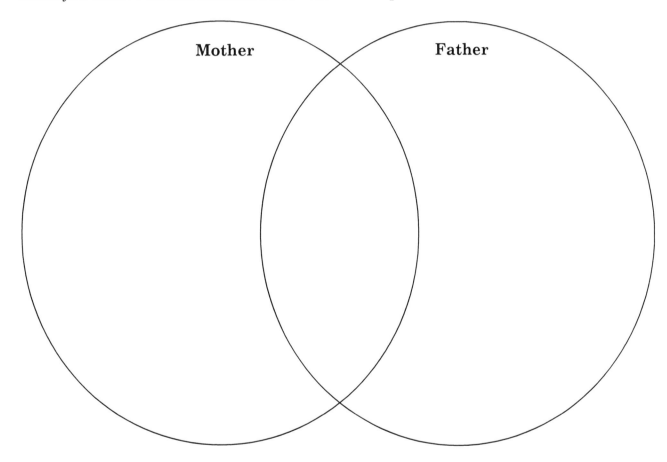

Writing Activity;

Write the letter you think Esther might have written to her father.

CHAPTERS 16 - 19

Vocabulary: Antonyms are words with opposite meanings. Draw a line from each word in column A to its antonym in column B. Then use the words in column A to fill in the blanks in the sentences below.

<u>A</u>	<u>B</u>
1. adamant	a. absent
2. ludicrous	b. scorn
3. ubiquitous	c. flexible
4. pessimist	d. temporary
5. effusiveness	e. reasonable
6. oblivious	f. optimist
7. indelible	g. reserve
8. reverence	h. worst
9. optimum	i. inability
10. proficiency	j. aware

. . . .

1. They called me a(n) _____ when I predicted rain for our entire vacation.

2. You cannot erase _____ ink.

3. My _____ with a hammer and saw leads me to believe I would make a good carpenter.

4. No matter how much I begged, my mother was _____ about not letting me stay out past midnight.

5. The book was so interesting that I became _____ to the noise and events taking place all around me.

6. It is _____ to expect every person you meet to become a close friend.

7. Despite traps and sprays, the _____ ants were turning our kitchen into a battle zone.

8. Sharing a(n) _____ for education, the young parents were determined to send each of their children to college.

9. The _____ of our family embarrassed the guest who was not accustomed to so many hugs and kisses.

10. Because of low mortgage rates, this is the _____ time to buy a house.

Chapters 16 - 19 (cont.)

Questions:

1. How did Yozia and Zaya help Mother keep her sanity? Why did Esther not need them quite as much?

2. How did Esther and her mother get a respite from cold and hunger? What problem did this present?

3. How did Raisa Nikitovna react when Esther expressed her wish to enter the declamation contest? Why did she react that way?

4. On the day of the contest, how did Esther find herself "together in a nightmare" with the character Tatyana?

5. How did Esther's new school compare to her old one?

6. Why did Esther go out one Sunday despite her mother's warning that a storm was coming? What disappointment did she encounter?

7. How did Esther's mother save her daughter's life?

8. Why did Uncle Yozia have Esther trade for him at the *baracholka*? Why did she have difficulty trading the book of Chekhov short stories?

9. Why was Esther able to excel in Anna Semyonovna's class?

Questions for Discussion:

1. What did Esther mean when she said, "reading was not only a great delight, but a *privilege*"? Have you ever felt the same way?

2. Why do you think that the declamation contest was so important to Esther?

3. Compare and contrast Raisa Nikitovna's and Anna Semyonovna's teaching methods. What do you think would have been the results of the declamation contest had Anna Semyonovna been in charge?

Literary Connection:

Obtain a copy of Pushkin's *Eugene Onegin* and read Tatyana's dream. What is your opinion of the work? Why do you think that Esther chose this piece to present in the declamation contest?

Chapters 16 - 19 (cont.)

Literary Devices:

I. *Metaphor* — What is being compared in the following metaphor?

> The world was a maniacal, gyrating black funnel of noise and I was in the bottom of it.

_____

Why is this an apt comparison?

_____

_____

II. *Building Suspense* — When we read a story, we become involved in its plot. We want to know what will happen next and how the story will end. This interest in the outcome of a story is called suspense. The author builds suspense by placing the characters in danger, leaving the reader uncertain of the outcome. In what ways does the author build suspense during the storm in Chapter Eighteen?

_____

_____

Writing Activity:

In a well-developed paragraph or two, tell about a teacher or other adult who had an important influence on your life.

CHAPTERS 20 - 22

Vocabulary: Analogies are equations in which the first pair of words has the same relationship as the second pair of words. For example: WIN is to LOSE as SMILE is to FROWN. Both pairs of words are opposites. Choose the best word from the Word Box to complete each of the analogies below.

> **WORD BOX**
>
> aspirations   bestiality   camaraderie   devastation
> invincible   pretext   solitude   wizened

1. ARGUMENT is to QUARREL as EXCUSE is to _____.

2. FRENZY is to COMPOSURE as _____ is to KINDNESS.

3. AMBITIONS is to _____ as FEELINGS is to EMOTIONS.

4. _____ is to WEAK as EXCITING is to TIRESOME.

5. CONTEMPT is to ADMIRATION as HOSTILITY is to _____.

6. SPIRITED is to LIVELY as _____ is to WITHERED.

7. ALONE is to _____ as SAD is to DEPRESSION

8. PROBLEM is to DIFFICULTY as RUIN is to _____.

Questions:

1. What different schemes did Esther use to get Yuri's attention?
2. Why did the theater company lend a gown to Yuri's escort at the ball after turning down Esther's request? How did this seem to belie Soviet doctrine?
3. How were the German prisoners treated in Siberia? Why were they treated this way?
4. After the war ended, what was "the most terrible news of all" for Esther and her family?
5. Why did Esther want to remain in Siberia?
6. Why did Father wish a sad farewell to Vilna?
7. Why did Esther become obsessed with obtaining a *sapogy* and a *fufaika*?

Chapters 20 - 22 (cont.)

8. How did the trip home on the cattle cars differ from the one that brought the deportees to Siberia?

9. Why did Esther think that Reiner's father was "the most noble man" she had ever met?

10. What happened to cause someone in the car to moan, "Not again, dear God in heaven, not again"? What effect did this have on Esther?

11. What made Esther realize that her *sapogy* and *fufaika* were not suited for her new life in Poland? How did this bring home the fact to Esther that her exile was over?

Questions for Discussion:

1. Do you think the inhumane treatment of the German prisoners of war in Siberia was justified?

2. What would you miss the most if a natural or political disaster deprived you of your home and possessions?

3. In what ways were Esther's determination an asset and a detriment to her during her family's exile?

4. What problems do you think await the Rudomin family as they try to make a new life for themselves? If you were the Rudomins, would you want to stay in Poland? Why or why not?

Literary Device: Symbolism

A symbol in literature is an object, person, or event that represents an idea or a set of ideas. What did the *sapogy* and the *fufaika* symbolize?

_____

_____

Social Studies Connection:

Esther and her family are very sad to hear about the death of President Franklin D. Roosevelt. Do some research to learn more about this President. Where and when was he born? What obstacles did he have to overcome? When did he become President? How long did he serve in office? What were his major accomplishments? Why was he such an important figure internationally?

Chapters 20 - 22 (cont.)

Literary Element: Conflict

The plot of a novel is the sequence of events that happen in the story. A conflict is a struggle between opposing forces. An *external conflict* is a character's struggle against an outside force, such as nature, fate, or another person. An *internal conflict* is a personal struggle that takes place within a character. In the chart below, list the conflicts that occurred in the story. Then indicate how these problems were resolved.

External Conflicts	Resolutions

Internal Conflicts	Resolutions

Writing Activities:

1. Imagine that you are a war correspondent. Write an article about the return of the deportees to Poland.

2. Imagine that you are Esther and write a letter to Shurik telling him about your return to Poland.

CLOZE ACTIVITY

The following passage has been taken from Chapter Eighteen of the novel. Read it through completely and then fill in each blank with word that makes sense. Afterwards you may compare your language with that of the author.

I was halfway home when I saw the first signs of danger. As far as the eye could see, all around, wherever I looked, _____[1] was lifting and spiraling from the steppe. _____[2] swirling mass of wind-driven snow is called _____[3] *buran*. The *buran* in itself, as it _____[4] from the steppe, is dangerous enough; with _____[5] whirlpools making one totally blind, it is _____[6] dangerous than falling snow. As I stood _____[7] for a second, I felt as if _____[8] whole huge steppe were revolving under my _____.[9] Then, as it does in Siberia in _____[10] great winter storm, the world went black. _____[11] wind blew up with a force that _____[12] me sideways, and now the snow was _____[13] both from the earth and from the _____.[14] The world was maniacal, gyrating black _____[15] of noise and I was in the _____[16] of it. Alone. Completely alone.

I started _____[17] fight my way through this storm. I _____[18] that if I panicked, if I went _____[19] circles, if I stopped altogether, I would _____.[20] It was as brutally simple as that. _____[21] people had died this way. One minute's _____[22] could be fatal.

I kept telling myself _____[23] push forward, push forward. But with the _____[24] knocking me every which way, I had _____[25] I could do to keep on my _____.[26] I was no longer certain that I _____[27] going forward. I had lost my sense of direction.

POST-READING ACTIVITIES

1. Return to the K-W-L chart that you began on page four of this study guide before you read *The Endless Steppe*. Complete column three of the chart using informa-tion you learned while reading the book.

2. Read the information about the author at the end of the novel. In your opinion, what is another period of Esther Hautzig's life that would make a good novel?

3. In a work of literature, theme is the author's message or central idea. Trace the following themes as they appeared throughout the story:
    *   courage of common people
    *   importance of family and friends
    *   resiliency of the human spirit
    *   prejudice

4. In your library, locate books about the period and places mentioned in *The Endless Steppe*. In these books, find photos that might represent various characters and scenes in the novel. Share these pictures with your classmates.

5. This novel explains the meaning of many Russian words. Create a glossary of these words and their meanings. Then write a few paragraphs about life in Siberia, using as many of these words as possible.

6. **Cooperative Learning Activity:** Work with a small cooperative learning group to discuss making *The Endless Steppe* into a film. Then do the following:
    *   List the scenes and events on which you want the film to focus. Indicate those scenes you want to omit and those you may want to add or change.
    *   Make a list of the types of music or actual musical works that you think would be good background for the various scenes you listed above.
    *   Cast the major roles with classmates or with famous actors of today.

7. The author takes great care to describe the clothing worn in Poland and Siberia at the time the novel takes place. Imagine that you are in charge of the costume design for the film proposed above. In the library, locate books containing photo-graphs and illustrations of the clothes described in the novel. Make copies of depictions of clothing you believe the characters should wear. Then, indicate which character should wear each particular outfit. You might want to cut and paste the copies into a collage that could serve as a costuming plan for a film production.

Post-Reading Activites (cont.)

8. With a small group of your classmates, role-play any of the following hypothetical scenes:

    - Grandmother Sara, Esther's maternal grandmother, and her Uncle Liusik comfort each other after members of their family are taken away on the trucks.

    - Esther's parents talk about their fears for their daughter in Siberia.

    - Raisa Nikitovna and Anna Semyonovna compare and contrast their philosophies of teaching and their opinions of Esther as a student.

    - Uncle Yozia and Aunt Zaya discuss how they can best help Esther and her mother.

    - Esther and her father catch up on the important events in their lives that occurred while they were parted.

9. Create a shoe box diorama showing a scene of your choice from the novel. You might wish to find photographs in books about this period in history to help you make your depiction as accurate as possible.

10. Esther enters a declamation contest. With your classmates, hold such a contest in your class. Ask your teacher to suggest selections that would make good oral presentations. Then all who wish to enter the contest should choose selections to present to the class. Have some students in the class act as judges to choose the winner or give a prize to each entrant.

11. Do some research in current newspapers and magazines to learn about Jews living in Poland today. Learn why so many young Poles are learning for the first time that they have Jewish ancestry.

SUGGESTIONS FOR FURTHER READING

Adler, David. *We Remember the Holocaust.* Holt.

Appleman-Jurman, Alicia. *Alicia: My Story.* Bantam.

Drucker, Malka, and Michael Halperin. *Jacob's Rescue.* Bantam.

* Frank, Anne. *Anne Frank: The Diary of a Young Girl.* Bantam.

Kerr, Judith. *When Hitler Stole Pink Rabbit.* Dell.

* Levitin, Sonia. *Journey to America.* Aladdin.

* Lowry, Lois. *Number the Stars.* Dell.

Richter, Hans Peter. *Friedrich.* Viking.

Roth-Hano, Renee. *Touch Wood.* Four Winds.

Sender, Ruth Minsky. *To Life.* Penguin.

Serraillier, Ian. *Escape from Warsaw.* Scholastic.

Siegal, Aranka. *Upon the Head of the Goat: A Childhood in Hungary.* Penguin.

Ten Boom, Corrie. *The Hiding Place.* Bantam.

* Wiesel, Elie. *Night.* Bantam.

* Yolen, Jane. *The Devil's Arithmetic.* Viking.

Some Other Books by Esther Hautzig

Cook Cooking: 16 Recipes Without a Stove. Morrow.

Let's Make Presents: 100 Gifts for Less Than $1.00. Crowell.

Redecorating Your Room for Practically Nothing. Crowell.

The Seven Good Years and Other Stories of I.L. Peretz. Jewish Publications Society of America.

* *A Gift for Mama.* Viking.

Holiday Treats. Simon & Schuster.

Remember Who You Are: Stories About Being Jewish. Crown.

* NOVEL-TIES Study Guides are available for these titles.

ANSWER KEY

Chapters 1, 2

Vocabulary: 1. e 2. c 3. h 4. a 5. d 6. i 7. f 8. b 9. j 10. g; 1. fetid 2. immaculate 3. fastidiously 4. opulent 5. incessantly 6. surreptitiously 7. aberration 8. explicit 9. sardonic 10. admonishing

Questions: 1. Esther enjoyed living in Vilna before the Russian soldiers arrived because she was the only child in a large, affluent, loving, extended family. She felt that the war did not penetrate the garden of her house. 2. Once Hitler's armies invaded Poland, Esther's family found itself caught in the middle of war, with Esther's father being drafted into the Polish Army; also, the Russians, who occupied Vilna, confiscated the family business and property. 3. Russian soldiers came to the house to arrest the family for being "capitalists." 4. Esther's mother forbid her daughter to take the photos because she was afraid they might help the Russians track down other members of the family. 5. Esther's grandmother screamed when Grandfather was told to board a different train from the rest of the family. Grandmother pleaded with a soldier to let her go with her husband. 6. Esther noticed that the overcrowded cars stank of animals and were as hot as a furnace. 7. On the first night in the cattle car, Esther slept; her Grandmother Anna wept; her father became a leader of the group and comforted his family; and her mother, refusing to cry, put all her effort into trying to maintain her composure. 8. Esther's mother revealed that she was a very proud individual. 9. In the cattle cars, the stench became worse; hunger was a problem since there was little food other than a revolting cabbage soup; and lice and disease were prevalent. 10. The journey lasted six weeks. At the end, there were no cheers; rather, the people silently gathered their belongings in a near frenzy, afraid that they might be left behind in the car.

Chapters 3 - 5

Vocabulary: 1. g 2. d 3. h 4. a 5. i 6. e 7. b 8. j 9. c 10. f; 1. austere 2. insinuated 3. deference 4. cataclysm 5. circumscribed 6. demeaning 7. bucolic 8. inadvertently 9. ostentatiously 10. malevolent

Questions: 1. Rubtsovsk was a frontier village built around a large open square in straight lines, surrounded by flat, desolate, treeless land. 2. Esther was stunned and alarmed when she learned that she was in Siberia. She had been taught that Siberia was a point of no return, where political prisoners endured cruel punishment and brutal weather. 3. Popravka was sarcastic and cruel, while Makrinin was kind and courteous. 4. Esther concluded that her family was luckier than others because they were not separated. 5. The friendly water boy showed deference to Esther's grandmother and treated the prisoners with respect; the girls stole a watermelon and cut it up to give to the prisoners. The effect of these acts of kindness was to make a dismal situation more tolerable for the prisoners. 6. Esther weeded the potato fields; her father drove a horse and buggy; her mother was in charge of women who were dynamiting; her grandmother shoveled the gypsum. Although Makrinin appreciated each family member's talents and shortcomings, he was forced to follow the irrational orders of his Soviet bosses. 7. At the baracholka, Esther felt free for the first time since she was arrested; she loved the sights and sounds of the market, which made her forget her troubles; she had a marvelous time trading. 8. Esther and her grandmother both enjoyed the gaiety of the baracholka; they were "born traders"; they both exhibited extremes of emotion: they were either very sad or very happy.

Chapters 6, 7

Vocabulary: 1. amnesty – general pardon for past offenses against a government 2. stipend – fixed or regular pay 3. hypocritically – insincerely 4. ingratiating – engaging 5. indulgent – kind or lenient 6. inaccessibly – in a way that is hard to get at 7. dossier – collection of papers about some subject or person 8. barrage – large number of words, blows, etc., coming quickly one after another

Questions: 1. Once amnesty was granted, the family was free to leave the mine and move closer to the village; and they would receive a small stipend for assigned work. The Rudomins still couldn't go home and had to endure the hard life in Siberia. 2. Esther meant that Anya defied the suffering she endured by keeping up her appearance against seemingly insurmountable obstacles. 3. The family now had *nari* with a straw pad as a bed, and there was one kerosene lamp in the room. 4. Esther wanted her family to move to the village so that she could attend school. 5. Nina did not believe that the Rudomins were Jews because she had been taught that all Jews had crooked noses and the men wore long beards. Never having met any

Jews before, Nina held fast to prejudices and stereotypes. 6. Esther was enchanted with the first snowfall because her family always loved snow back home. Esther's parents worried how Esther would survive the winter without proper clothes. 7. School turned out to be a disappointment because one of Esther's teachers, Raisa Nikitovna, was very severe; Svetlana, the girl with whom Esther had to share a book, was unfriendly; and not knowing Russian well, Esther found that she had trouble keeping up with the lessons. 8. In the school Esther attended, the curriculum was molded by post-revolutionary politics. Whole segments of history were omitted, such as any mention of the last Tsar and his family. Works of literature were also selected to illustrate Soviet principles.

Chapters 8 - 11

Vocabulary: Across — 1. paroxysms 4. dexterously 10. largesse 11. infirmary 12. pilfering 13. incongruously 14. egregious; Down — 2. amenities 3. superfluous 4. dour 5. taciturn 6. obliterating 7. cajole 8. reminiscent 9. pariah

Questions: 1. When Esther suggested they go to the police, Mrs. Kaftal's face turned red, and she trembled from head to toe. Grandmother covered up the crime because she didn't want to embarrass Mrs. Kaftal by openly accusing her. 2. Esther could not go to school when she came down with bronchitis. The Russian doctor was a kind, competent physician who really cared about her patients. 3. Esther's first personal confrontation with tragedy came upon learning of the death of her grandfather. A sad time was made even worse because the police interrupted the ritual mourning; Grandmother had to sit *shivah* alone; and she did not have the *yahrzeit* candle to burn during the mourning period. 4. The Rudomins had to move because Nina was expecting a baby and there would be no room for them in the hut. It was harder now to find new housing because more and more Russians were escaping to Siberia as the Germans penetrated further into Russia. 5. Unlike Nina's clean, cheerful hut, the new home was a crowded room in a dirty, bug-infested, dingy, little hut. 6. Esther's father was detained and interrogated by the secret police. When they asked him to spy on all the deportees, he refused, saying they could shoot him. 7. Esther felt less like an outsider after she was invited to go with two girls to an American movie; and when Svetlana became her friend after she cut off her braids, which the Russian girl had envied. 8. The Rudomins left the dour sisters' hut because it became unbearably stifling in the summer and the inhabitants irritated one another. Esther thought that the new hut that the family fixed up for themselves was wonderful because she had privacy and more space. 9. Vanya changed from a quiet, friendless outcast to a friendly man who carried himself with dignity. When the Rudomin family treated him with kindness and respect, he slowly responded.

Chapters 12 - 15

Vocabulary: 1. nondescript 2. degradation 3. magnitude 4. woebegone 5. atrocities 6. infraction 7. opaque 8. revulsion

Questions: 1. Other than going to school, the children hauled bricks back and forth in wheelbarrows, dumping them down and picking them up, supposedly helping the war effort; they also helped out at nearby collective farms. 2. Esther's father was ordered to work in a labor brigade near the front lines. Esther's father tried to comfort his family; Esther was distraught; Esther's mother uncharacteristically wept and Grandmother took the news in stride. 3. The family's greatest concern was hunger during the winter since their crop had yielded few potatoes and it would be very hard to obtain food. 4. To supplement the family's fuel supply, Esther stole coal and wood shavings. Mother and Grandmother knew that survival came before any code of honor in Siberia. 5. Esther's mother made her daughter a surprise party to cheer her up after her father's departure and a bout of flu, and perhaps to remind herself that there were still good things in life. It was both a happy and a sad occasion for the family: happy because they were able to laugh and have a festive occasion in Siberia, but sad because Father wasn't there on the day that was also his wedding anniversary. 6. Mother and Grandmother were worried about their family back in Poland because the war news was full of stories about German atrocities. Esther's mother regretted not having identified her brother to the Russian soldiers back in Vilna so that he could be with her now. 7. Since the thirty rubles was the only money that the family had, Esther thought its loss would be translated to starvation. Esther's mother did not punish her because she was more concerned with her daughter's feelings than with money. 8. Esther's first customer was a crippled woman who wanted Esther to knit a sweater for her little girl. Esther was filled with pride when she completed her first project. 9. Marya took advantage by asking Esther to make a sweater out of a filthy, badly torn skirt for only a bag of flour, a pail of potatoes, and some liters of milk; when the finished sweater

was too small because Marya gained weight, the woman made the girl redo it without further payment. This behavior revealed Marya as a selfish person who cared little about the troubles of others.

Chapters 16 - 19

Vocabulary: 1. c 2. e 3. a 4. f 5. g 6. j 7. d 8. b 9. h 10. i; 1. pessimist 2. indelible 3. proficiency 4. adamant 5. oblivious 6. ludicrous 7. ubiquitous 8. reverence 9. effusiveness 10. optimum

Questions: 1. Yozia and Zaya helped Mother keep her sanity by offering her civility, friendship, good talk, and culture, thus reminding her of her old life. Esther had the occupation of her schoolwork and the companionship of her friends to take her mind off her troubles. 2. Yozia got Esther and her mother a temporary position caring for Yosif Isayevich, a tractor factory director, in his comfortable home. Since Grandmother couldn't go with them, she had to stay with the Kaftals. 3. Raisa was sarcastic and scornful when Esther expressed her wish to enter the declamation contest. Raisa did not think a Polish deportee should be allowed the same privileges as a Soviet citizen. Grandmother suggested her attitude was based on anti-Semitism. 4. On the day of the contest, Esther was reciting a poem about Tatyana's nightmare; meanwhile, she was living her own nightmare by giving a poor recitation because she had been forced to run back to her hut to get shoes. 5. At Esther's new school, the children treated her as an outsider, and it was more than an hour's walk each way; on the other hand, the school was warm and had excellent teachers. 6. Esther disobeyed her mother because she had finished her knitting for Alexandra Lvovna and wanted to be paid. When the woman wouldn't pay until she herself got paid for the dress, Esther was extremely disappointed. 7. Esther's mother went outside and recited a prayer to guide Esther home. Esther heard her voice in the blinding storm and knew she was near home. 8. Knowing that he could not just give her money, Uncle Yozia gave Esther items he didn't need to trade at the *baracholka*. She could then keep half the profits. Esther had difficulty trading a collection of Chekhov's short stories, especially when she realized that the peasants wanted to buy it to use the paper to roll cigarettes. 9. Esther was able to excel in Anna Semyonovna's class because she taught with passion and regarded her students with respect. She also realized that Esther had a special need, and excellent intellectual capacity. This caused a friendship to grow between them which made Esther try even harder in her class.

Chapters 20 - 22

Vocabulary: 1. pretext 2. bestiality 3. aspirations 4. invincible 5. camaraderie 6. wizened 7. solitude 8. devastation

Questions: 1. To get Yuri's attention, Esther became editor of the school paper; she sought tutoring from a woman who lived near Yuri; and she tried to borrow a gown for a ball to attract Yuri. 2. Esther, being a deportee, had no status, and would not be lent a gown, while the daughter of the head of the factory had influence and was granted her request. This seemed to belie the Soviet concept of a classless society. 3. The German prisoners were starved, enslaved, and treated with contempt. They were treated this way in revenge for German atrocities that had been committed. 4. The terrible news at the end of the war was that all the members of the Rudomin family, except for two cousins and an aunt, had been killed by the Germans. 5. Esther wanted to remain in Siberia because it had become her home and she was afraid of change. She also was wary of returning to Vilna where nothing would be the same. 6. Vilna, which was now part of Soviet-controlled Poland, was occupied by Russian officials and sympathetic Poles who now lived in the best homes, such as the Rudomin's family home. When Father was freed, he returned to Vilna briefly to find a changed, looted city that was now under the control of strangers. He sadly visited the graves of his ancestors and relatives and left. 7. Esther wanted to take some of the world she knew back to an uncertain world as protection. 8. The trip home was filled with joy. This time the doors were not locked—the deportees were not prisoners. 9. Esther thought Reiner's father was the most noble man she had ever met because he did not reproach Esther for being the cause of his son's absence from the train. 10. When some of the Poles observed the cattle cars, they cursed at the Jews inside and threw stones. Esther was frightened and bewildered to see the people she had idolized acting this way. 11. Esther's father commented that they must get her some new clothes. Esther realized that the last tangible manifestations of her life in Siberia must be put aside for her new life in Poland.